Did You Know?
WEST YORKSHIRE

A MISCELLANY

Compiled by Julia Skinner

With particular reference to the work of Alan Brooke,
Clive Hardy, Lesley Kipling, Robert Preedy and Roly Smith.

THE FRANCIS FRITH COLLECTION

www.francisfrith.com

First published in the United Kingdom in 2010 by The Francis Frith Collection®

This edition published in 2014
ISBN 978-1-84589-829-8

Text and Design copyright The Francis Frith Collection®
Photographs copyright The Francis Frith Collection® except where indicated.

The Frith® photographs and the Frith® logo are reproduced under licence from
Heritage Photographic Resources Ltd, the owners of the Frith® archive and trademarks.
'The Francis Frith Collection', 'Francis Frith' and 'Frith' are registered trademarks of
Heritage Photographic Resources Ltd.

All rights reserved. No photograph in this publication may be sold to a third party other than in the original
form of this publication, or framed for sale to a third party. No parts of this publication may be reproduced,
stored in a retrieval system, or transmitted, in any form, or by any means, electronic, mechanical, photocopying,
recording or otherwise, without the prior permission of the publishers and copyright holder.

British Library Cataloguing in Publication Data

Did You Know? West Yorkshire - A Miscellany
Compiled by Julia Skinner
With particular reference to the work of Alan Brooke, Clive Hardy, Lesley Kipling,
Robert Preedy and Roly Smith

The Francis Frith Collection
6 Oakley Business Park,
Wylye Road, Dinton,
Wiltshire SP3 5EU
Tel: +44 (0) 1722 716 376
Email: info@francisfrith.co.uk
www.francisfrith.com

Printed and bound in England

Front Cover: **KEIGHLEY, LOW STREET c1910** K60506p
Frontispiece: **BOSTON SPA, HIGH STREET 1893** 32000

The colour-tinting is for illustrative purposes only, and is not intended to be historically accurate

AS WITH ANY HISTORICAL DATABASE, THE FRANCIS FRITH ARCHIVE IS CONSTANTLY BEING
CORRECTED AND IMPROVED, AND THE PUBLISHERS WOULD WELCOME INFORMATION ON
OMISSIONS OR INACCURACIES

CONTENTS

- 2 Introduction
- 5 West Yorkshire Dialect Words and Phrases
- 6 Haunted West Yorkshire
- 8 West Yorkshire Miscellany
- 42 Sporting West Yorkshire
- 46 Quiz Questions
- 48 Recipes
- 52 Quiz Answers
- 54 Francis Frith - Pioneer Victorian Photographer

Did You Know?
WEST YORKSHIRE
A MISCELLANY

INTRODUCTION

West Yorkshire was the powerhouse for the industrialisation of woollen and textile manufacturing, and in the 18th and 19th centuries this region was at the forefront of a global trade in textiles. Places such as Leeds, Bradford, Halifax and Huddersfield developed along the fast-flowing rivers which originally gave power to their mills. The combination of the factory system and later the application of steam power to the textile mills led to the concentration of textile production in a handful of towns, and much of the vast wealth that the textile industry created was invested in the splendid civic buildings which abound in the towns and cities of this area.

Towards the end of the 17th century the spinning of worsted yarn gained a foothold around Halifax and Bradford, and in the 18th century both the spinning of worsted yarn and the manufacture of worsted cloth became major industries in Bradford. Worsted cloth, also known in the past as 'stuff', is lightweight with a hard, smooth texture, and is cooler to wear than woollen cloth made by other processes. By the 19th century Bradford had become the centre of the woollen and worsted industry throughout the world. Its Wool Exchange was home to 3,000 dealers, with buyers and sellers trading wool from West Yorkshire, the Colonies and the Far East (see photograph 39512 on page 49). The 19th-century skyline at Bradford would have been a forest of mill chimneys, but there were also other industries, as well as a large manufacturing base which grew up in Bradford to support the textile mills and machinery. Many of the textile mills and some heavier industries have now closed down, but the story of the days when Bradford was the woollen capital of the world is told at the Bradford Industrial Museum in a former spinning mill at Eccleshall, where the attractions include working machinery, textile workers' cottages, and the mill owner's house.

By the 18th century Leeds was not only a centre for the manufacture of woollen cloth but had also become the leading finishing centre in the region for cropping, dyeing and dressing cloth. Daniel Defoe visited Leeds in the 1720s and reckoned that in a morning, cloth was traded in the open-air cloth market at Leeds to the value of between £10,000-£20,000. By 1710 open-air cloth markets were being challenged by Cloth Halls, where business could be done inside, whatever the weather. Leeds had two such halls, for White Cloth and a Mixed (Coloured) Cloth Hall; Leeds Post Office was built on the site of the Mixed Cloth Hall in 1896. Although Leeds was originally a 'wool' town, by the mid 19th century factories in the area moved into ready-made clothing and tailoring, and by the beginning of the 20th century Leeds was the world centre for that trade – Montague Burton's mill was the largest clothing manufactory in the world in the 1920s. Bobbins and shuttles still fly at Armley Mills Industrial Museum in Leeds, vividly illustrating the working lives of many local people in the heyday of the city's textile industry.

Did You Know?
WEST YORKSHIRE
A MISCELLANY

As the Industrial Revolution developed, mechanisation was viewed with suspicion by many workers in the old cottage industries of textile manufacture, who feared for their jobs. The fear manifested itself in Luddism; the Luddites fought against technical innovation, and textile mills were attacked, machinery was destroyed and manufacturers were threatened. A particularly famous incident occurred at Huddersfield in 1812, when the government poured troops into the area to quell the unrest, and some Luddites were executed. The workforce also began to change, with much use made in the manufactories of female and child labour; hand weaving was considered a man's job in the old cottage industry system and power looms did not make much of an impression in Yorkshire's textile factories until the 1820s and 1830s, but once their advantages were seen they soon became widespread in the industry, enabling women and girls to weave. The prospect of work in Yorkshire's textile mills attracted thousands of people from all over Britain to the rapidly expanding industrial towns and cities.

By the end of the 20th century, West Yorkshire's textile industry was in decline against foreign competition and economic forces. Mills were closed, thousands of jobs were lost, and the physical appearance of the region's towns and cities was transformed as the textile mills and their landmark chimneys disappeared. Although vestiges of the textile and other associated industries remain, the way of life and the rich culture they sustained are gone forever, replaced by new industries for the modern age. Working in the mills was often a hard life which took its toll in accidents and disease, but there is no doubt that it engendered a strong sense of community, and that people felt great pride in their work.

WEST YORKSHIRE DIALECT WORDS AND PHRASES

'A brussen tup' – someone who is full of his own importance.
'Addling brass' – earning money.
'Agate' – to be busy or occupied with something.
'Ah'm sad flayed' – I'm a bit stupid.
'Baht' – without.
'Brussen' – burst, as in a bag bursting.
'Cal' – gossip.
'Causey' – pavement.
'Clammed' – cold, also used to mean hungry.
'Dollypawed' – left-handed.
'Get agate then' – get on with it.
'Ginnel' – a narrow passageway between buildings.
'Goit' – a channel cut to carry water to a mill.
'Featherlegged' – very tired.
'Fettle' – to clean something, or to put it in good order.
'Fuzzock' – a donkey.
'Lake' – idle.
'Leit green' – crafty, cunning.
'Lumb' – a chimney.
'Moudiwarp' – a mole.
'Muckment' – rubbish, refuse.
'Mullock' – a mess or a muddle.
'Sackless' – lazy.
'Saig' – a saw, thus **'saigins'** meaning sawdust.
'Shauve' – a slice of bread.
'Shuck' – crazy.
'Throng' – busy.
'Tyke' – the broad Yorkshire dialect.

HAUNTED WEST YORKSHIRE

The historic Shibden Hall in Halifax is said to be one of the town's most haunted buildings. A former curator reported seeing a cat 'walk through' the wall of her office, and other staff have reported mysterious scents, such as lavender and pipe tobacco. Perhaps the most haunted pub in Halifax is the Ring 'o' Bells in Upper Kirkgate, where the unexplained scent of lavender has been noticed, as well as the smell of burning. Staff have reported switches being mysteriously turned off, and taps being turned on in the night when there is nobody there. There have also been several reports of a ghostly man seen standing near the fire in the pub, often accompanied by the smell of pipe smoke.

Be careful if you walk on Castle Hill at Huddersfield at night – people have reported hearing the sounds of fighting and phantom horses galloping past them to a ghostly battlefield. The station in St George's Square in Huddersfield is said to be haunted by the ghost of a railway porter called Jonah who was hit by a train and had to retire because of his injuries. The sound of his spiteful laughter can be heard whenever there is an accident on the site.

A number of ghosts roam East Riddlesden Hall at Keighley. A Grey Lady who glides up the stairs, along the landing and into a bedroom is believed to be the shade of a former lady of the house whose husband discovered her with her lover; he locked her into her bedroom, where she starved to death. Her lover was bricked-up in a room and left to die, and years ago the room was found, complete with a man's skeleton; a ghostly face which has been seen looking out from the Rose Window of the hall is said to be his.

There are several ghost stories linked with Leeds. The City Varieties Theatre is said to be haunted late at night by the ghost of a mysterious piano player. A small prison beneath Leeds Town Hall, the Bridewell, is said to be haunted by the ghost of Charlie Peace, a violent thief and double murderer who was held there before his trial and execution at Armely Prison in 1879. The old gatehouse of Kirkstall Abbey, now the Abbey House Museum, is reputedly haunted by the ghost of a former abbot.

A famous ghost story from Bradford comes from the time of the Civil War, when the town was held for Parliament and was besieged by the Royalist forces of the Earl of Newcastle. During the siege the Earl stayed at Bolling Hall, which was then outside the town. The story goes that the Earl was so enraged by the resistance of the people of Bradford that one night he went to bed declaring that when the town was taken, he would slaughter every man, woman and child in the place. He woke during the night to see a ghost standing beside him, wringing its hands and moaning 'Pity poor Bradford!'. The experience shook the Earl so much that he changed his plans, deciding only to attack those who resisted him. Bradford eventually fell to the Earl, who kept his word.

An old folklore belief in the Leeds area was that the souls of babies who died before they were baptised would return to haunt their parents, in the shape of devil dogs known as Gabble Retchets.

Several ghosts are said to haunt the Tudor-Jacobean mansion of Temple Newsam near Leeds. The Blue Lady is believed to be the shade of Mary Ingram, whose portrait hangs above the fireplace in the Green Damask Room. She was robbed by a highwayman while returning home by carriage one night, and afterwards became obsessed with hiding her possessions. The ghostly Blue Lady has been reported apparently frantically searching for something, presumably her lost belongings. Another ghost, a White Lady, is said to be that of Lady Jane Dudley who fell in love with Lord Darnley, born at Temple Newson, who married Mary, Queen of Scots. Lady Jane's love for Lord Darnley was not reciprocated, and she hanged herself when she heard of his betrothal to the queen. Other ghosts at Temple Newsam are said to be a monk, a Knight Templar and a small boy. Many strange phenomena at the house have also been reported, such as the sensation of something pushing past people on the stairs, an unexplainable 'misty form', and the sound of screaming coming from the South Wing.

The moors around Ilkley are full of ancient monuments and rocks carved with ancient symbols, and there are many legends and ghost stories linked with the area. One is that a spectral black hound known as the Barguest roams the moors above Ilkley and Otley, especially near the Cow and Calf rocks; sightings of the ghostly hound portend doom.

WEST YORKSHIRE MISCELLANY

West Yorkshire comprises most of the old West Riding area, which originally extended down to Sheffield. It was the Viking Danes who first divided the huge county of Yorkshire into the ridings, or 'thridings' (thirds), and they became the North, East and West Ridings before local government reorganisation in 1974.

One of Bradford's prominent businessmen in the 19th century was Samuel Cunliffe Lister, after whom Lister Park was named, who built the magnificent Manningham (or Lister's) Mill, now converted into apartments. Its tall chimney, known as 'Lister's pride', is a prominent landmark. In 1891 Bradford's mill workers went on strike for almost five months against a reduction in wages at Lister's mill due to a fall-off in orders. They eventually returned to work having gained nothing, but a direct result of the strike was the founding of the Independent Labour Party at a conference held in Bradford in 1893. Among those present was Keir Hardie, who became the first Labour Member of Parliament in 1900.

In the 19th century all workers who handled wool or animal hair and hides were at risk of catching the deadly disease of anthrax. These products were an important part of Bradford's trade and industry, and the disease became so prevalent amongst its workers that anthrax at one time was known as the Bradford Disease. In the 1890s Frederick William Eurich was appointed to work in a laboratory in the Technical College and investigate the disease. After years of experiments which put himself in considerable danger, Eurich found that the disease was transferred to humans when they came into contact with blood from an infected animal. The use of formaldehyde and rigorous precautions and inspection of wool and other fibres led to a decrease in cases of anthrax, and in later years the development of antibiotics provided a cure for the disease. Eurich was awarded the Gold Medal of the Textile Institute in recognition of the thousands of lives in the textile industry that were saved as a result of his work.

BRADFORD, A TRAM IN TYRRELL STREET 1903 49713a

In the 1850s Titus Salt built a state-of-the-art mill and model industrial village for his workers which he called Saltaire, then three miles outside Bradford. Provision was made for welfare benefits and help was given to the aged, infirm and sick, but Saltaire had no pubs – Titus Salt was firmly against alcohol. The modern Italianate mill at Saltaire was the largest in Europe: the weaving shed housed 1,200 looms and a workforce in excess of 3,000. The tall chimney of the mill in 1909 can be seen in the background of photograph 21024, (page 45). The mill closed as a textile manufactory in 1986, but the building now incorporates shops, art galleries and industrial units for high-tech businesses.

Photograph 39506x (opposite) shows the statue of Richard Oastler, 'The Factory King', in its original position in Forster Square in Bradford; it now stands on North Parade. Richard Oastler fought against the use of child labour in the industrial mills in the 18th and 19th centuries. Many of these children were sent north from London workhouses. In the early days of the Industrial Revolution, those who ended up in the mills around Leeds were luckier than the children sent to Bradford: in Leeds they only had to work a 12-hour day, against a 13-hour day in Bradford. Even children as young as five were sometimes expected to work these hours.

Forster Square in Bradford was named after the Bradford Member of Parliament W E Forster, 'The Education King', who sponsored the Elementary Education Act of 1870, which provided free state education to children aged between 5 and 12. The area around Forster Square became known as 'Little Germany' after large numbers of Germans came to Bradford in the Victorian era and established warehouses there.

Did You Know?
WEST YORKSHIRE
A MISCELLANY

BRADFORD, FORSTER SQUARE 1897 39506x

BINGLEY, LOCKS ON THE LEEDS AND LIVERPOOL CANAL c1900
B98501

The Industrial Museum at Moorside Mills in Bradford has several cars in its collection made by Bradford's Jowett Car Company, which was founded in 1910 by Benjamin and William Jowett and ceased production in 1954. The company was famous for the Bradford van, and the Jowett Javelin and Jupiter cars.

One of Bradford's famous literary sons was the author and playwright J B Priestly, born in Mannheim Road in 1894 and educated at Belle Vue Boys' School. He later moved to London, but was involved in the founding of the Bradford Civic Theatre, which now commemorates him in its new name of The Priestley Centre for the Arts.

At 127 miles in length, the Leeds and Liverpool Canal was the longest in Britain. The five rise locks on the canal near Bingley are one of the wonders of the waterway system (photograph B98501, above). They are known as staircase locks, because the top gate of each chamber is also the bottom one of the next: there is no water between the two.

Did You Know?
WEST YORKSHIRE
A MISCELLANY

In the 19th century the three literary Brontë sisters, Charlotte, Emily, and Anne, and their brother Bramwell, lived in the parsonage at Haworth, where their father Patrick was vicar of the church of St Michael and All Angels. The wild moorland landscapes around Haworth surely gave the Brontë sisters the inspiration for their novels, the most famous of which are 'Jane Eyre', 'Wuthering Heights' and 'The Tenant of Wildfell Hall'. Haworth is now a place of literary pilgrimage, where The Parsonage Museum provides an insight into the sisters' lives and works.

HAWORTH, THE BRONTE PARSONAGE MUSEUM c1955 H194023

KEIGHLEY, THE CATTLE MARKET c1910 K60504

Keighley was recorded as 'Cichhelai' in the Domesday Book of 1086. The name is believed to have meant either 'Cyhha's Farm', or 'Cyhha's Clearing'. In former times Keighley was known for its cattle markets, and its Beast Fairs were held twice a year, in May and November, right in the centre of town in Russell Street. At the close of business the local fire brigade would be called in to hose the mess off the streets!

In 1744 a man by the name of John Shires discovered a saline spring, Boston Spa was born, and for a few years this was the fashionable place to be seen. A stagecoach service operated on a daily basis from Leeds and back, and wealthy travellers using the Great North Road would stop over and sample the delights of the pump room. Boston Spa never achieved the fame of other Yorkshire spa towns like Ilkley and Harrogate, but the buildings on its High Street illustrate the affluence generated for a while by the town's sulphurous, saline water with purgative qualities.

Did You Know?
WEST YORKSHIRE
A MISCELLANY

For centuries the town of Wetherby was an important stopping place on the Great North Road, being exactly halfway between London and Edinburgh. It is now the starting point for the annual Great Yorkshire Bike Ride in June, a seventy-mile ride for charity which starts at Wetherby Racecourse and ends at Filey on the east Yorkshire coast.

WETHERBY, NORTH STREET 1909 61731

Did You Know?
WEST YORKSHIRE
A MISCELLANY

KIRKSTALL ABBEY, THE WESTERN FACADE c1861 7411

The ruined Kirkstall Abbey near Leeds is one of the finest and most complete examples of early Cistercian architecture in Britain. The main entrance to the abbey church was through the imposing porch seen in photograph 7411, opposite, enriched with capitals with scalloped details; the original circular window above was replaced by the two round-arched windows in the late 15th century. After the Dissolution, the abbey was left a ruin, but the chapter house, cloisters and abbot's lodging are still impressive. The gatehouse is now the Abbey House Museum, showing life in Leeds in the 19th century.

Following the Norman Conquest, Leeds was a small village under the lordship of Ilbert de Lacy, William the Conqueror's deputy in that region of England, and so appears to have escaped the king's wrath when he laid waste much of Yorkshire following uprisings against Norman rule in the northern lands in 1069-70. The people of this area were lucky: King William's reprisals were savage, and it has been estimated that one third of the West Riding villages were destroyed. Symeon of Durham wrote of William's 'Harrying of the North', describing the devastation wrought on towns, villages and farmsteads, and of the corpses left to rot where they had fallen.

The centrepiece of City Square in Leeds is the statue of the 14th-century Edward of Woodstock, known as the Black Prince. It was commissioned by the Lord Mayor, Thomas Walter Harding, to celebrate Leeds achieving city status in 1893, but the Black Prince had no connection at all with Leeds. However, there are four other statues in City Square of people who did have some connection with Leeds, or an influence on its development. They are statues of: Dr Walter Farquhar Hook, Bishop of Leeds; James Watt, inventor, whose steam engines were a major factor in the Industrial Revolution; Joseph Priestley, a scientist who was born near Leeds, who made important discoveries about oxygen; and John Harrison, a wealthy local worthy and benefactor of the 17th century.

Did You Know?
WEST YORKSHIRE
A MISCELLANY

LEEDS, THE TOWN HALL 1894 34765

Did You Know?
WEST YORKSHIRE
A MISCELLANY

The Town Hall at Leeds with its magnificent many-pillared clock tower was designed by the Hull architect Cuthbert Broderick, who also designed the city's wonderful Corn Exchange with its domed glass roof and the Mechanics' Institute, later the Civic Theatre. Built between 1853 and 1858, this sumptuous public building was deliberately ambitious in scale, its dignified and spectacular classical lines symbolising the reputation of Leeds as a leading city of the West Ridings.

Did You Know?
WEST YORKSHIRE
A MISCELLANY

The name for an inhabitant of Leeds is a 'loiner', from the word 'loin' for a roll of cloth, thus a reference to Leeds as a centre of the cloth trade in the past, but by the mid 19th century there was an enormous diversity in the manufacturing base of Leeds. Woollens still dominated the scene, but the flax industry employed over 9,000 workers, and other industries included rope, glass, earthenware and paper manufacturing, engineering and iron founding. Another major industry in the area was coalmining; at its height there were 102 local collieries, employing 5,000 miners. In the 19th century the Leeds area became a centre for the manufacture of railway locomotives. The last of the Leeds locomotive builders to remain in business was the Hunslet Engine Co, surviving into the 1990s.

LEEDS, THE POST OFFICE AND REVENUE OFFICE 1897 39088

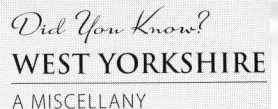
Did You Know?
WEST YORKSHIRE
A MISCELLANY

To mark the Millennium a new statue was commissioned for Leeds, sited on the Eastgate Roundabout. Local people voted to choose the subject for the work, and the final choice was for it to commemorate Arthur Aaron VC, a young airman and graduate of Leeds University who died in the Second World War. He was posthumously awarded the Distinguished Flying Medal and the Victoria Cross after his death in 1943. The 5m-high bronze statue shows the young airman with children from the period 1950-2000 climbing up a tree; the highest and smallest child is releasing the dove of peace.

Now a suburb of Leeds, Headingley was in the Wapentake of Skyrack in the past, an ancient name for an administrative area. The word 'skyrack' is believed to have derived from 'Scir ac', the 'Shire Oak' under which meetings were held. This historic tree collapsed in 1941, but is recalled in the names of two local pubs, the Original Oak and the Skyrack.

By 1890, Cleckheaton in the Spen valley was the world centre of card clothing, the making of a device (a sheet of leather inset with wire teeth) to comb wool prior to being spun. Before the machines were invented to do the job, women and children as young as four set the wire teeth, and were paid half a penny for every 1400 teeth carded.

Yorkshire's coal fields brought great wealth to the county, but there were also tragedies associated with the industry. For instance, in the church of St Mary Magdalene in Altofts, near Normanton, is a memorial window commemorating 32 men and boys (and 53 horses) who were killed in the explosion at the West Riding Colliery on 2nd October 1886.

Did You Know?
WEST YORKSHIRE
A MISCELLANY

HAREWOOD, HAREWOOD HOUSE c1886 7365

Halfway between Leeds and Harrogate is Harewood House, one of Yorkshire's finest stately homes. It was designed by Robert Adam and John Carr (see page 27), and the north front of the house was remodelled in 1843 by Sir Charles Barry. The house contains many treasures, including an unrivalled collection of 18th-century furniture made especially for Harewood by the great furniture designer Thomas Chippendale, who was born at Otley, also in West Yorkshire. Hidden within the estate of Harewood House is the exterior set of the 'Emmerdale' village, where much of the TV series is filmed.

The magnificent Palladian stately home of Nostell Priory near Wakefield also holds a fine collection of furniture by Thomas Chippendale, which was specially made for the house. Chippendale is believed to have also made some of the furniture in the delightful 18th-century dolls' house that can be seen at Nostell Priory.

Did You Know?
WEST YORKSHIRE
A MISCELLANY

The lovely market town of Otley was the birthplace in 1718 of the furniture designer Thomas Chippendale. Wesley Street in Otley is named after the Methodist preacher John Wesley, who was a frequent visitor to the town; there is a local tradition that his horse died in Otley on one of his visits and is buried in the grounds of the parish church, marked by an unusually-shaped stone known as 'the Donkey Stone'.

In the 1880s the railway station at Normanton became a staging post for immigrants on their long journey from Scandinavia to Liverpool and then to America. Over 700,000 passengers passed through Normanton each year, and the station employed around 700 staff. Normanton declined when other lines offered a quicker service, but it still retained maintenance services for locomotives like the Flying Scotsman.

OTLEY, KIRKGATE c1960 O49041

HUDDERSFIELD, ASPLEY BASIN 2005 H151702

The growth of Huddersfield into one of the most important textile towns in Britain can be traced back to 1671, when John Ramsden obtained a market charter from Charles II. Huddersfield was at the junction of two river valleys, had good access to Leeds, Bradford and Halifax, and was on the trans-Pennine routes. By the mid 18th century local clothiers were part of an international trade with markets all over Britain and overseas. The Ramsdens tapped into this expanding trade, building the Cloth Hall in 1766 and later opening the Ramsden Canal which connected Huddersfield, via the Calder Navigation, to Goole and Hull. The arrival of the railway ushered in Huddersfield's coming of age as an industrial town, and the second half of the 19th century saw further growth, not only of the town's textile industry but the other industries that it helped generate; Huddersfield engineering and chemical firms were amongst those leading the country.

In the background of photograph H151702 (opposite) of Aspley Basin at Huddersfield, the local landmark of Castle Hill can be seen, topped with the tower which was built to commemorate Queen Victoria's Diamond Jubilee of 1897.

In 1841 two Huddersfield gunmakers, William Golden and John Hanson, patented a breech loading needle gun. They claimed that this was the weapon (usually attributed to von Dreyse) which was adopted by the Prussian army and helped change the course of European history. In 1866 Hanson exhibited one of the original guns at Folly Hall.

During the Second World War, engineers Thomas Broadbent & Sons of Huddersfield secretly built four midget submarines known as X Craft which were used in the Normandy landings in 1944.

The Town Hall at Todmorden, built in 1870, once stood on the border between Yorkshire and Lancashire, a fact reflected in the carvings in the pediment frieze on its classical front: there are bales of cotton on the western (Lancashire) side and wool on the eastern (Yorkshire) side. Pevsner compared this fine Town Hall to that of Birmingham. Todmorden, or 'Tod' as it is always known locally, is now firmly in West Yorkshire.

The Calder Valley of Yorkshire is famous for its Dock Pudding, which is fried in bacon fat and eaten for breakfast or supper. The plant used is not the common dock, however, but bistort, or sweet dock, which is similar to spinach. It grows in the early spring, and so in former years it was a useful food plant as it provided some fresh greens during the time of the year known as the 'hungry gap', when winter food stores were running out and not much else was yet ready to harvest. A traditional Dock Pudding also contained nettles, wild garlic and oatmeal. The tradition is remembered in the World Dock Pudding Championships which are held every April or May in Mytholmroyd in the Calder Valley.

HUDDERSFIELD, THE RAILWAY STATION AND THE STATUE OF HAROLD WILSON 2005 H151738

The George Hotel in St George Square in Huddersfield was built in 1850 by Joseph Kaye, a local merchant and mill owner, to accommodate railway travellers. He also contracted Huddersfield's impressive station, whose classic grandeur still dominates St George's Square (photograph H151738, above) – a great achievement for a man who could barely write his own name. Designed by the architect J R Prichett, Huddersfield Railway Station with its massive Corinthian columns is justly claimed to have the most magnificent station façade in the country.

Cluntergate in Horbury, near Wakefield, was the birthplace of the famous 18th-century architect John Carr, who was twice Mayor of York and worked on Harewood House. His father, Robert, was a local stonemason and quarry owner, and young John started his training in his father's quarry. John Carr is buried in the crypt of the parish church of St Peter and St Leonard at Horbury, which he designed and had built himself.

Did You Know?
WEST YORKSHIRE
A MISCELLANY

Beneath the clock tower of the Town Hall at Ossett is the town's motto: 'Inutile Utile ex Arte', which means 'useless things are made useful by skill', and accurately describes the industry that allowed the town to flourish: its woollen mills later specialised in recycling old rags to feed the local works, as old clothes and fabrics were torn apart and reprocessed to begin life again as new textiles. Recycled rags mixed with virgin wool made 'shoddy', and 'mungo' was when tailors' clippings of cloth were mixed into the process. In 1912 Ossett had 90 rag merchants and 18 shoddy and mungo factories. Other major centres of the 'shoddy' industry in the past were Batley and Dewsbury, which re-used old woollen items to make heavy woollens such as blankets and military uniforms.

HORBURY, CLUNTERGATE c1955 H214017

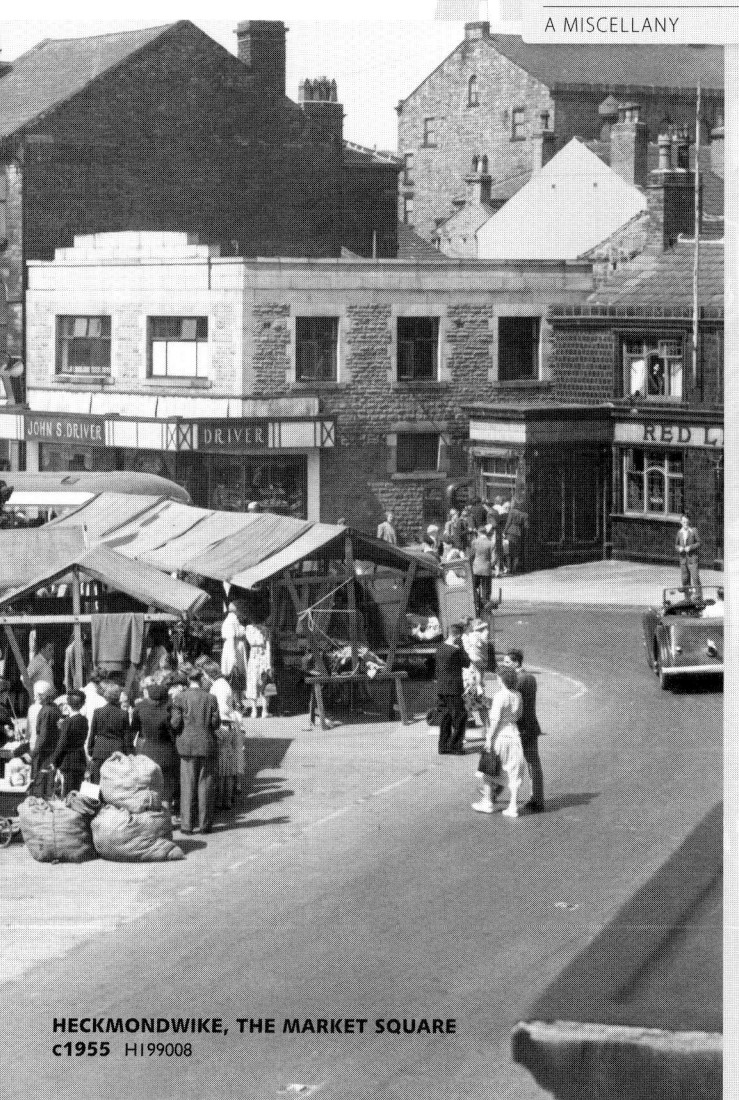

Did You Know?
WEST YORKSHIRE
A MISCELLANY

**HECKMONDWIKE, THE MARKET SQUARE
c1955** H199008

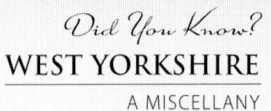

Did You Know?
WEST YORKSHIRE
A MISCELLANY

The famous old packhorse bridge seen in photograph H198016 (below) gave the town of Hebden Bridge its name. Known as 'the Pennine Centre', in the past Hebden Bridge was the meeting point of packhorse routes from Halifax to Heptonstall, Burnley and Rochdale. Many of the old houses which backed onto Hebden Water and several of the woollen mill chimneys have now gone, and the area seen in this view has now been opened up as a riverside park. Hebden Bridge is known for its 'double decker' housing that was built up the steep sides of the valley around the town as its textile industry developed with the coming of the Rochdale Canal, and later the railway, to the area.

HEBDEN BRIDGE, THE OLD PACK HORSE BRIDGE c1955 H198016

WAKEFIELD, CROSS SQUARE c1955 W464019

Many of Wakefield's street names are reminders of its history: along Bread Street, for instance, a bakehouse was established in 1306 and all bakers had to use this communal oven; in the Middle Ages, water ran from a muddy field near the centre of today's city, where the road nowadays is called the Springs; and Wakefield's market cross stood at the head of Cross Street from 1707 to 1866. The city's mercantile past can be seen in the rich architecture all around the centre, as the prosperity that came to Wakefield in the 19th century enabled its merchants to build grand new houses and developments. Wood Street contains the municipal reflection of this affluence, with the old Mechanics' Institute, the Town Hall, the Court House and the West Riding County Hall, all built in the 19th century. Wakefield's parish church of All Saints attained cathedral status in 1888. The oldest part dates from 1329, whilst its spire, at 247 feet, is the highest in Yorkshire.

Did You Know?
WEST YORKSHIRE
A MISCELLANY

In 1903 the famous sculptor Barbara Hepworth was born at number 15 Duke Street in Wakefield, and her work is displayed in the Art Gallery and near County Hall in the city. Five years earlier, in 1898, another world-famous sculptor, Henry Moore, was born at 30 Roundhill Road in Castleford, the son of a local miner. In Henry Moore's day Castleford would have been a noisy and smoky place, as the town at this time was surrounded by massive collieries and glass works. The river was central to this activity, with barges towing 'Tom Puddings' wending their way in non-stop processions up and down the waterway. 'Tom Puddings' were short containers that could be coupled together in any length. When they reached their destination, they were lifted with a hoist and turned upside down so that the coal could be emptied out – just like a pudding being turned out from a pudding bowl. A barge hauling coal loaded onto 'Tom Puddings' can be seen near the power station near Knottingley in photograph K82038, below.

KNOTTINGLEY, THE POWER STATION c1955 K82038

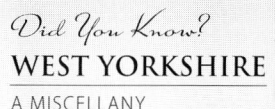
Did You Know?
WEST YORKSHIRE
A MISCELLANY

After the Norman Conquest a wooden castle was built at Pontefract, which was later rebuilt in stone. The Civil War of the 17th century put an end to this stronghold: in 1649, at the end of its third siege supporting Charles I, the castle was forced to surrender and Parliament ordered its demolition.

The prosperous Georgian feel of Pontefract derives from its historic role as a market town and agricultural centre: the name of Beastfair in the town centre recalls the cattle market which used to be held there. Other local trades in the past included stone quarrying, rope making and mining: the Prince of Wales pit at Tanshelf opened in 1870 and by 1931 employed 19,000. Pontefract's largely 18th-century Market Place was formerly known as the Shambles, the area of town where meat was sold. A landmark in the town is the Buttercross, built in 1734 (shown in photograph P155024 on page 50), where local farmers' wives would come to sell their dairy produce.

The Crusaders of the 12th century probably introduced the liquorice plant to Pontefract, and from that grew a hugely important industry; it still flourishes today, but the liquorice roots are no longer grown locally. The disc-shaped sweets flavoured with liquorice known as Pontefract Cakes (or 'Pomfret' or 'Pomfrey' Cakes) are still made in the town, and an annual liquorice festival is held there, where liquorice-flavoured cheese, ice-cream and beer can be sampled. Liquorice is known as 'Spanish' in some parts of Yorkshire.

The small town of Holmfirth in the Holme Valley is now famous as the location for the long-running TV comedy 'Last of the Summer Wine'. But even before Compo and Co arrived, Holmfirth was famous as the home of the comic seaside postcards produced by the Bamforth company, which was also an early pioneer of the British film industry.

Did You Know?
WEST YORKSHIRE
A MISCELLANY

HALIFAX, THE PIECE HALL c1995 H9701

Did You Know?
WEST YORKSHIRE
A MISCELLANY

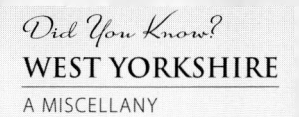

Set in the foothills of the Pennines, Halifax is one of the great cloth towns of England and has been a producer of cloth since the 13th century. In the 19th and early 20th centuries Halifax was the greatest of the textile towns of West Yorkshire, a centre for woollen manufacture and clothing that was larger even than Leeds or Bradford. Photograph H9701 (opposite) shows a modern view of the famous and historic Piece Hall in Halifax, completed in 1779. This superb Italianate building was where wool merchants traded and weavers sold their pieces of cloth in 315 small rooms on three storeys, built around a quadrangle. The Piece Hall in Halifax, which has been described as the most impressive example of industrial architecture in the north of England, is the only complete 18th-century cloth market building in Yorkshire.

Halifax is often known as 'Toffee Town'. It was here that John Mackintosh invented his famous toffee in the 1890s, a cross between traditional English toffee which was rock hard and American toffee in the soft caramel style. He and his wife first sold the toffee from their pastry shop at King Cross. John Mackintosh's company merged with Rowntree of York in 1988, but his most famous creation is still popular – Quality Street.

It was in Halifax in the 1930s that Percy Shaw patented 'cat's eyes', or to give them their proper name, reflecting road studs, and produced them at his company in the town. James May, a presenter on BBC TV's 'Top Gear', said of Mr Shaw's simple but effective invention that "this little block of iron and rubber has probably done more to save lives on the road than anything since".

Did You Know?
WEST YORKSHIRE
A MISCELLANY

The Town Hall at Halifax, in the background of photograph H9001 (below), was designed in the Italian style by Sir Charles Barry, and is notable for its extraordinary-looking clock tower. Described as a cross between a Renaissance palace and a medieval cathedral, the Town Hall opened at the head of Princess Street in 1863. The central Victoria Hall had a splendid stone and marble floor covered in a tasteful Crossley carpet provided by the one-time Mayor John Crossley, the town's biggest carpet manufacturer.

HALIFAX, TOWN HALL 1900 H9001

Did You Know?
WEST YORKSHIRE
A MISCELLANY

ILKLEY, THE GROVE 1911 63556

Although Ilkley's origins are in Roman times, when a fort was established in the area, its development really took off in the mid 19th century, when it became a popular spa town; soon Ilkley was claiming to be 'the Malvern of the North'. Above the town, Ilkley Moor is rich in archaeological remains, including many intriguingly carved rocks. By the Bronze Age (1500-500BC) people were carving strange cup-and-ring patterns on a number of rocks near the town, which are unique to this area. Overlooking Ilkley is the Swastika Stone, so called because of its engraved design, the outline of a swastika (or fylfot), which is thought to date from the Iron Age. The swastika, infamous now thanks to its 20th-century associations, is in fact an ancient design found all over the world and is believed to be a symbol for good fortune, or perhaps fertility.

Ilkley's famous Saxon crosses are shown in the graveyard of All Saints' Church in the 1870s in photograph 7290 (opposite); they are now preserved inside the church tower. The central pillar dates from AD850, and features carvings depicting the four Gospel writers of the New Testament, the saints Matthew, Mark, Luke and John.

The Darwin Gardens Millennium Green in Ilkley is named after Charles Darwin, who was visiting a hydropathic establishment in the town in 1859 when his book 'On the Origin of Species' was published. The Darwin Gardens Millennium Green features monuments and art works with an evolutionary theme.

'On Ilkla Moor Baht'at' ('On Ilkley Moor Without a Hat') – so where did that famous Yorkshire song come from? The tune is from the hymn 'Cranbrook'. In 1886 a church choir from Halifax was holding its summer picnic on the moors near Ilkley. One of the young girls, Mary Jane, wandered off with her sweetheart. When the couple returned, the rest of the choir teased them by bursting into song with new words to the tune: 'Where's tha bin since Ah saw thee? Tha's been a-courting Mary Jane'.

OPPOSITE: **ILKLEY, ALL SAINTS' CHURCH, THE SAXON CROSSES IN CHURCHYARD c1874** 7290

Did You Know?
WEST YORKSHIRE
A MISCELLANY

Did You Know?
WEST YORKSHIRE
A MISCELLANY

Did You Know?
WEST YORKSHIRE
A MISCELLANY

ILKLEY, COW AND CALF ROCKS c1874 7281

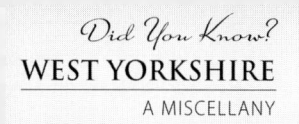

SPORTING WEST YORKSHIRE

Rugby League was founded at a meeting at the George Hotel in Huddersfield in 1895, when twenty-two clubs met and formed the NRFU (Northern Rugby Football Union) as a breakaway group from the RFU (Rugby Football Union). This revolution in the world of rugby was sparked by the RFU's decision to enforce the amateur principle of the sport. The NRFU became the Rugby Football League in 1922.

Halifax RLFC, originally formed in 1873, was one of the original twenty-two rugby clubs that formed the NRFU in 1895. Halifax RLFC share The Shay Stadium with Halifax Town FC; this is the largest ground in England to be used by a non-league football club, but in the 1960s it attracted the lowest attendance ever recorded for a professional English football match, when Halifax Town played Millwall.

Bradford Northern Rugby League Club was the first club after the Second World War to reach three successive Wembley Challenge Cup finals – in 1947, 1948 and 1949. Odsal Stadium, home of the club, for many years held the world record for attendance at a Rugby League match. 102,569 people officially attended the Challenge Cup Final replay between Halifax and Warrington in May 1954, although it was thought by many observers that the actual attendance was over 120,000.

Rugby players moving between the two codes in deals involving large sums of money are fairly commonplace nowadays, but Leeds Rugby League Club was a long way ahead of its times when it amazed the rugby world by paying a record fee of £6,000 for Llanelli Union star Lewis Jones in 1952. The move eventually paid rich dividends when the team won its first League Championship in 1961 under Jones's captaincy.

The home of Yorkshire County Cricket Club is at Headingley, near Leeds. The very first cricket match played here in 1890 was between Leeds and Scarborough, and in the same year a North of England XI entertained the Australian team. Yorkshire County matches transferred to the ground from the previous county pitch at Sheffield – in the first Yorkshire cricket game in 1891, the home team lost to Derbyshire by 45 runs. Test cricket came in 1899, and rugby was first played here in 1895 by Leeds FC, one of the original clubs that formed the Rugby League. The Headlingley stadium is unusual because it is effectively two grounds, for both cricket and rugby, unified by a stand which has one side facing the cricket pitch and one side facing the rugby pitch. Both grounds regularly host international fixtures. The rugby ground is home to two teams, the Leeds Rhinos Rugby League team, and the Leeds Tykes Rugby Union team. Leeds Tykes Rugby Union Club is a relatively young club, formed from an amalgamation of clubs in Roundhay and Headingley. Over the years, the two old clubs produced at least 40 international players, including Peter Winterbottom, who became only the second player to appear 50 times for England.

Huddersfield Town Football Club won the FA Cup in 1922 and became the first club to win the League Championship three times in a row, in 1923/24, 1924/25 and 1925/26. The legendary Bill Shankley became manager of Huddersfield Town FC in 1956. One of his notable signings for the club was the 15 year-old Denis Law, who went on to find fame as a Scottish international and Manchester United star. When Law was sold to Manchester City four years later for what was then a new British record transfer fee of £55,000, some of the money was used to finance the new floodlights at the Leeds Road ground, which became known as the 'Denis Law Lights'.

The famous and successful Leeds United Football Club of the late 1960s and early 1970s was notable for the continuity in its playing staff. Six players from this era made over 700 appearances for the club – Jack Charlton and Billy Bremner both played on 773 occasions – and three more players made more than 500 appearances.

A name from West Yorkshire in football history is that of Albert Geldard, who was 15 years and 158 days old when he made his debut for Bradford Park Avenue Football Club in 1929, and held the record as the youngest player ever to play League football until it was broken in the 2008/09 season by Barnsley Football Club's Reuben Noble-Lazarus. Albert Geldard also represented England before his 20th birthday.

The origins of Bradford City AFC were in Manningham Rugby League Club. In 1903 the club switched to association football, and without having played a game were invited to join the Football League. This was an attempt to introduce soccer into a rugby-dominated area, and City were the first West Riding club in the League. By 1911 the club had reached the first division and won the FA Cup. Bradford City's unusual colours of claret and amber are distinctive, and City scarves are popular with fans of the 'Harry Potter' books, as they are also the colours of Hogwarts' School. Coincidentally, Bradford City actually had a player called Harry Potter before the First World War!

Since its formation as a 'super club' in 1963, City of Leeds Swimming Club has enjoyed great success in producing international medal winners. These have included Adrian Moorhouse, who won Olympic gold, Andy Astbury, who won Olympic bronze, and two World Championship winners, James Hickman and Claire Huddart. The club has won the National Club Championship on many occasions.

The 1960 Olympic swimming champion Anita Lonsbrough was born in Huddersfield in 1941 and worked at the Town Hall as a clerk. At the age of 19 she won a gold medal in the 200m breaststroke event at the 1960 Olympics in Rome in a thrilling final in world record time, and received a hero's welcome on her return home to Huddersfield. At one time in her career she held not only the Olympic gold medal but also the Empire and European gold medals at the same time. She also made sporting history by becoming the first woman to win the BBC Sports Personality of the Year award in 1962, and was the first woman to carry the flag for the British team at the Olympics, at Tokyo in 1964.

Did You Know?
WEST YORKSHIRE
A MISCELLANY

Ilkley Tennis Club's annual Open Tournament is one of the premier competitions in the North of England, and includes an international men's tennis event as well as an LTA tournament for national standard juniors. Another local event is the five-mile Ilkley Moor Fell Race, staged by the Ilkley Harriers Athletics Club. It is a challenging category 'Short A' fell race, but the popular event attracts a great number of fell runners every February. Ilkley is also famous as the place 'where Colin Montgomerie learnt his golf', as Ilkley Golf Club's website proudly proclaims – Montgomerie lived at Ilkley as a schoolboy, during which time he learnt to play at the town's beautiful golf course.

SALTAIRE, THE MILL AND THE CRICKET PITCH 1888 21024

Did You Know? WEST YORKSHIRE
A MISCELLANY

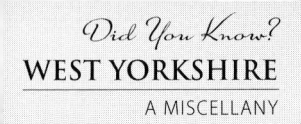

QUIZ QUESTIONS

Answers on page 52.

1. What were known as 'blind backs' in Leeds in the past?

2. Which famous chain of High Street shops started on a market stall in Leeds in 1884?

3. Which famous artist was commissioned to paint Huddersfield in 1965?

4. The British Prime Minister Harold Wilson (1916-1995) was born and educated in Huddersfield. He served two terms as Prime Minister, from 1964 to 1970, and again from 1974 to 1976. A statue of Huddersfield's famous son now stands in front of the town's railway station (photograph H151737, opposite). He was famously fond of an item of clothing made in West Yorkshire – what was it, and where was it made?

5. Bradford's City Hall is adorned at the second floor level with 35 statues of Kings and Queens of England and the United Kingdom – except for that of one person. Who is it?

6. The Cartwright Memorial Hall in Bradford was designed to hold the city's art treasures, but who is it named after, and what was his contribution to Bradford?

7. Which place in West Yorkshire is so magnificent that it has been called 'The Hampton Court of the North'?

8. The Old Bridge at Ilkley is recognised as the official starting point for which long-distance walk?

9. Why might you need earplugs on Christmas Eve if you live in Dewsbury?

10. What is the origin of the old Yorkshire saying 'From Hull, Hell and Halifax, good Lord deliver us'?

Did You Know?
WEST YORKSHIRE
A MISCELLANY

HUDDERSFIELD, THE STATUE OF HAROLD WILSON 2005 H151737

RECIPE

WEST RIDING PUDDING

> 175g/6oz shortcrust pastry
> 2 tablespoonfuls of raspberry jam
> 115g/4oz butter
> 115g/4oz caster sugar
> 2 eggs, beaten
> 115g/4oz self-raising flour
> 25g/1oz ground almonds
> Grated zest of half a lemon

Pre-heat the oven to 180°C/350°F/Gas Mark 4, and place a baking tray in the oven to heat up.

Roll out the pastry on a lightly floured surface, and use it to line a greased 20cm (8 inch) pie tin. Spread the base of the tart with raspberry jam.

Cream the butter and sugar together in a bowl until the mixture is light and fluffy. Beat in the eggs a little at a time, adding a little flour if necessary to prevent curdling. Sift the flour into the mixture, then add the ground almonds and grated lemon zest, and gently fold it all in.

Turn the mixture into the pie tin and spread it over the jam. Place the pie tin on the baking tray in the pre-heated oven and bake for 25-30 minutes, until the filling is well risen and firm and the pastry is golden and crisp. (Placing the pie tin on the pre-heated baking tray will help the pastry base to cook thoroughly.)

**BRADFORD, THE WOOL EXCHANGE
1897** 39512

Did You Know?
WEST YORKSHIRE
A MISCELLANY

Did You Know?
WEST YORKSHIRE
A MISCELLANY

**PONTEFRACT, ST GILES'
CHURCH AND BUTTERCROSS
1964** P155024

Did You Know?
WEST YORKSHIRE
A MISCELLANY

RECIPE

YORKSHIRE PARKIN

In the West Riding of Yorkshire it was traditional to eat parkin on Bonfire Night, 5th November. The black treacle gives this the true dark parkin colour.

> 300ml/ ½ pint milk
> 225g/8oz golden syrup
> 225g/8oz black treacle
> 115g/4oz butter or margarine
> 50g/2oz dark brown sugar
> 450g/1 lb plain flour
> Half a teaspoonful of bicarbonate of soda
> 1½ teaspoonfuls of ground ginger
> 350g/12oz medium oatmeal
> 1 egg, beaten

Pre-heat the oven to 180°C/350°F/Gas Mark 4.

Put the milk, syrup, treacle, butter or margarine and sugar into a saucepan and heat gently, stirring all the time, until the mixture has melted and is smooth. Take care not to let the mixture boil. When it has mixed together, take it off the heat and leave to cool for a few minutes. Put the flour, bicarbonate of soda, ginger and oatmeal into a large bowl and mix together. Make a well in the centre, pour in the beaten egg, then gradually pour in the milk and syrup mixture, stirring all the time, until it has formed a smooth batter.

Grease a 20cm (8 inch) square cake tin, and line the bottom with greaseproof paper. Pour the batter into the tin. Bake in the pre-heated oven for about 45 minutes, until the surface of the parkin is firm to the touch. Allow the parkin to cool in the tin for a few minutes, then turn out on to a wire rack to cool completely. Cut into pieces when cool, and store in an airtight tin, preferably leaving it for 3 days before eating to allow the parkin to become sticky.

QUIZ ANSWERS

1. One feature of the housing that was built for the industrial workers of Leeds in the past was the style of houses known as 'blind-backs', which had no rear windows or doors. From the end elevation they looked like a house that had been cut in half with one half pulled down.

2. Marks & Spencer. The Lithuanian immigrant Michael Marks opened his first Penny Bazaar stall in Leeds in 1884, selling buttons, wool, socks and stockings, before moving to Skipton where he co-founded Marks and Spencer with Tom Spencer.

3. L S Lowrie. His painting can be seen in Huddersfield Art Gallery.

4. Harold Wilson was noted for his partiality for Gannex raincoats, which were made in the West Yorkshire mill town of Elland in the Calder Valley.

5. Oliver Cromwell. Although he ruled the country, it was as Lord Protector, not as King.

6. It was named in memory of Dr Edmund Cartwright, who invented the power loom that brought so much wealth to Bradford.

7. Temple Newsam, a grand Tudor-Jacobean house near Leeds, is often dubbed 'The Hampton Court of the North'. It is now an important museum and art gallery.

8. The Old Bridge at Ilkley is the official starting point of the Dales Way, a long-distance walk through the Yorkshire Dales and across England to Lake Windermere in the Lake District.

9. A local custom at Dewsbury is for a bell of the parish church called 'Black Tom' to be rung on Christmas Eve, with a toll for every year of the Christian era. This means that the bell is now rung over 2,000 times; as the tolling has to finish at midnight, it currently begins just after 10pm.

10. The cloth industry was so important to Halifax in medieval times that the town was granted its own laws for dealing with people convicted of stealing cloth; those found guilty were beheaded on a guillotine-like contraption called the 'Halifax Gibbet'. The Halifax Gibbet Law, combined with the harsh anti-vagrancy laws of Hull, gave rise to the saying 'From Hull, Hell and Halifax, good Lord deliver us'.

HALIFAX, THE OLD GIBBET H9095

FRANCIS FRITH

PIONEER VICTORIAN PHOTOGRAPHER

Francis Frith, founder of the world-famous photographic archive, was a complex and multi-talented man. A devout Quaker and a highly successful Victorian businessman, he was philosophical by nature and pioneering in outlook. By 1855 he had already established a wholesale grocery business in Liverpool, and sold it for the astonishing sum of £200,000, which is the equivalent today of over £15,000,000. Now in his thirties, and captivated by the new science of photography, Frith set out on a series of pioneering journeys up the Nile and to the Near East.

INTRIGUE AND EXPLORATION

He was the first photographer to venture beyond the sixth cataract of the Nile. Africa was still the mysterious 'Dark Continent', and Stanley and Livingstone's historic meeting was a decade into the future. The conditions for picture taking confound belief. He laboured for hours in his wicker dark-room in the sweltering heat of the desert, while the volatile chemicals fizzed dangerously in their trays. Back in London he exhibited his photographs and was 'rapturously cheered' by members of the Royal Society. His reputation as a photographer was made overnight.

VENTURE OF A LIFE-TIME

By the 1870s the railways had threaded their way across the country, and Bank Holidays and half-day Saturdays had been made obligatory by Act of Parliament. All of a sudden the working man and his family were able to enjoy days out, take holidays, and see a little more of the world.

With typical business acumen, Francis Frith foresaw that these new tourists would enjoy having souvenirs to commemorate their days out. For the next thirty years he travelled the country by train and by pony and trap, producing fine photographs of seaside resorts and beauty spots that were keenly bought by millions of Victorians. These prints were painstakingly pasted into family albums and pored over during the dark nights of winter, rekindling precious memories of summer excursions. Frith's studio was soon supplying retail shops all over the country, and by 1890 F Frith & Co had become the greatest specialist photographic publishing company in the world, with over 2,000 sales outlets, and pioneered the picture postcard.

FRANCIS FRITH'S LEGACY

Francis Frith had died in 1898 at his villa in Cannes, his great project still growing. By 1970 the archive he created contained over a third of a million pictures showing 7,000 British towns and villages.

Frith's legacy to us today is of immense significance and value, for the magnificent archive of evocative photographs he created provides a unique record of change in the cities, towns and villages throughout Britain over a century and more. Frith and his fellow studio photographers revisited locations many times down the years to update their views, compiling for us an enthralling and colourful pageant of British life and character.

We are fortunate that Frith was dedicated to recording the minutiae of everyday life. For it is this sheer wealth of visual data, the painstaking chronicle of changes in dress, transport, street layouts, buildings, housing and landscape that captivates us so much today, offering us a powerful link with the past and with the lives of our ancestors.

Computers have now made it possible for Frith's many thousands of images to be accessed almost instantly. The archive offers every one of us an opportunity to examine the places where we and our families have lived and worked down the years. Its images, depicting our shared past, are now bringing pleasure and enlightenment to millions around the world a century and more after his death.

For further information visit: www.francisfrith.com

INTERIOR DECORATION

Frith's photographs can be seen framed and as giant wall murals in thousands of pubs, restaurants, hotels, banks, retail stores and other public buildings throughout Britain. These provide interesting and attractive décor, generating strong local interest and acting as a powerful reminder of gentler days in our increasingly busy and frenetic world.

FRITH PRODUCTS

All Frith photographs are available as prints and posters in a variety of different sizes and styles. In the UK we also offer a range of other gift and stationery products illustrated with Frith photographs, although many of these are not available for delivery outside the UK – see our web site for more information on the products available for delivery in your country.

THE INTERNET

Over 100,000 photographs of Britain can be viewed and purchased on the Frith web site. The web site also includes memories and reminiscences contributed by our customers, who have personal knowledge of localities and of the people and properties depicted in Frith photographs. If you wish to learn more about a specific town or village you may find these reminiscences fascinating to browse. Why not add your own comments if you think they would be of interest to others? See **www.francisfrith.com**

PLEASE HELP US BRING FRITH'S PHOTOGRAPHS TO LIFE

Our authors do their best to recount the history of the places they write about. They give insights into how particular towns and villages developed, they describe the architecture of streets and buildings, and they discuss the lives of famous people who lived there. But however knowledgeable our authors are, the story they tell is necessarily incomplete.

Frith's photographs are so much more than plain historical documents. They are living proofs of the flow of human life down the generations. They show real people at real moments in history; and each of those people is the son or daughter of someone, the brother or sister, aunt or uncle, grandfather or grandmother of someone else. All of them lived, worked and played in the streets depicted in Frith's photographs.

We would be grateful if you would give us your insights into the places shown in our photographs: the streets and buildings, the shops, businesses and industries. Post your memories of life in those streets on the Frith website: what it was like growing up there, who ran the local shop and what shopping was like years ago; if your workplace is shown tell us about your working day and what the building is used for now. Read other visitors' memories and reconnect with your shared local history and heritage. With your help more and more Frith photographs can be brought to life, and vital memories preserved for posterity, and for the benefit of historians in the future.

Wherever possible, we will try to include some of your comments in future editions of our books. Moreover, if you spot errors in dates, titles or other facts, please let us know, because our archive records are not always completely accurate—they rely on 140 years of human endeavour and hand-compiled records. You can email us using the contact form on the website.

Thank you!

For further information, trade, or author enquiries
please contact us at the address below:

The Francis Frith Collection, Unit 6, Oakley Business Park, Wylye Road, Dinton, Wiltshire SP3 5EU.
Tel: +44 (0)1722 716 376 Fax: +44 (0)1722 716 881
e-mail: sales@francisfrith.co.uk **www.francisfrith.com**